Oh, Look!
A Squirrel!

Planner & Journal

This journal belongs to:

....

Oh, Look!
A Squirrel!

Planner & Journal

 How to use this journal:

1. Use the Mind Map to creatively determine what to focus on.

2. Clip out pictures or sketch drawings to add to your vision board to keep you motivated.

3. Write out the top 5 goals you'd like to accomplish and refer back to this regularly.

4. Use the morning/evening routine pages to log the things you need to do at certain times or in certain situations. There are extra pages so that when you need to make adjustments, you can replace these lists with new ones.

5. Fill out the calendar with birthdays, appointments and milestones. Choose a daily habit to focus on and check the "H" box each day you perform the habit.

6. Each week has a space to reflect on the previous week and set goals for the upcoming week.

7. Each week has a "long list". Whenever you think of something you either need to do, want to do, or might do, you'll immediately write it on your "long list" so you don't forget it.

8. Under "today's priorities" you'll list only the tasks that absolutely must be done that day. By the end of that day, this stuff must be completed.

If you finish all items on your priority list before your evening routine begins, then add new items from your "Long List" to your priority list, but only if you will complete them that day.

9. Use the "calendar tasks" section to write in appointments from your calendar.

10. Use the blank pages at the end of this journal to jot down thoughts, musings and ideas.

MY 5 MOST IMPORTANT GOALS:

GOAL

GOAL

GOAL

GOAL

GOAL

I TRIED TO FOCUS MY ATTENTION.SO I STARTED TO MAKE A LIST, THEN I REALIZED I FORGOT TO PAY SOME BILLS, SO I GOT ONLINE AND SAW A MESSAGE FROM A FRIEND SO I GOT ON FACEBOOK AND...OH LOOK, A SQUIRREL!

morning
routine

TIME	ACTIVITY	NOTES

evening
routine

TIME	ACTIVITY	NOTES

morning
routine

TIME	ACTIVITY	NOTES

evening
routine

TIME	ACTIVITY	NOTES

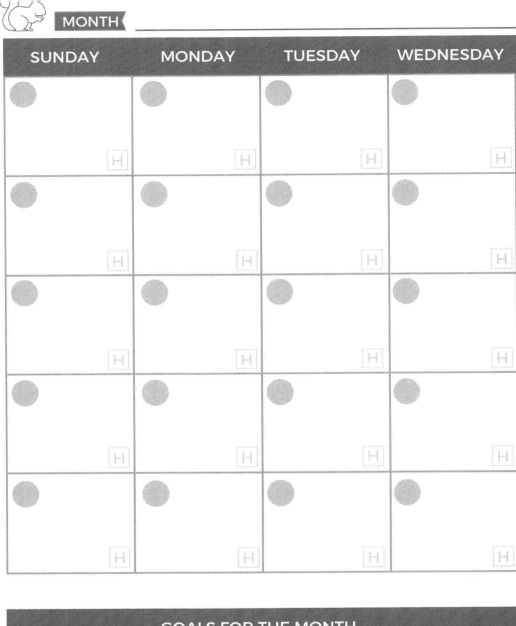

MONTH _____

SUNDAY	MONDAY	TUESDAY	WEDNESDAY
H	H	H	H
H	H	H	H
H	H	H	H
H	H	H	H
H	H	H	H

GOALS FOR THE MONTH

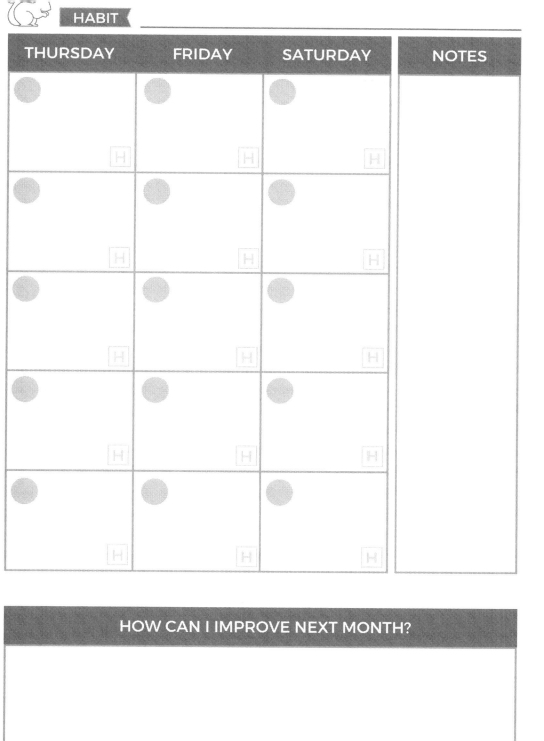

THURSDAY	FRIDAY	SATURDAY	NOTES
H	H	H	
H	H	H	
H	H	H	
H	H	H	
H	H	H	

HOW CAN I IMPROVE NEXT MONTH?

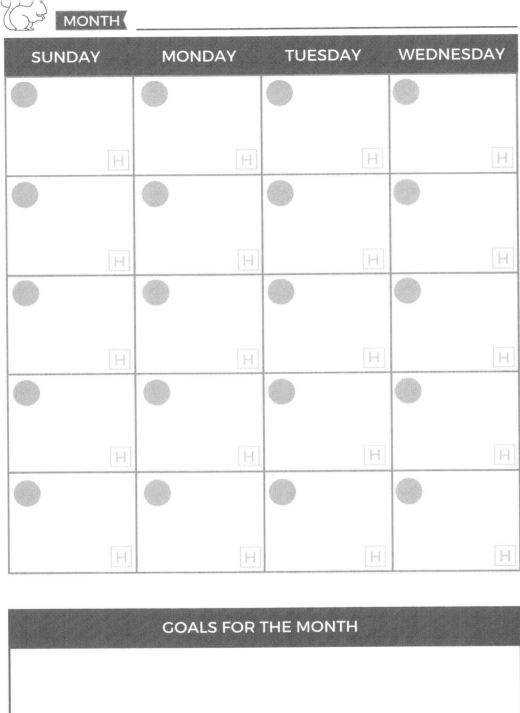

SUNDAY	MONDAY	TUESDAY	WEDNESDAY
H	H	H	H
H	H	H	H
H	H	H	H
H	H	H	H
H	H	H	H

GOALS FOR THE MONTH

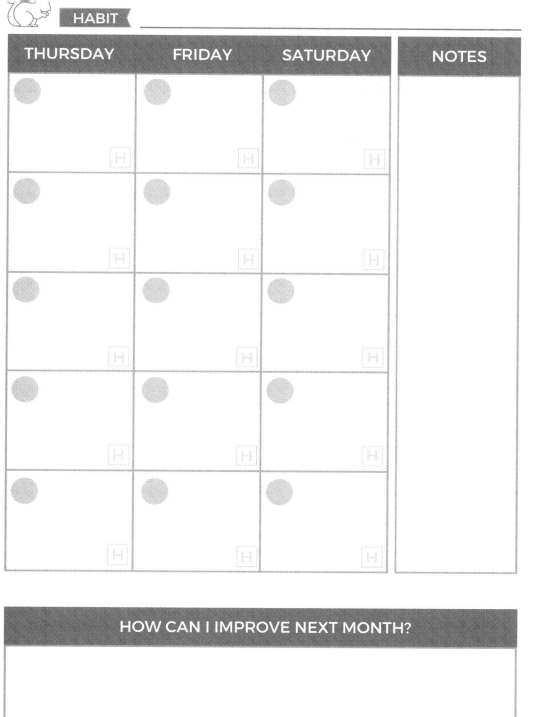

THURSDAY	FRIDAY	SATURDAY	NOTES

HOW CAN I IMPROVE NEXT MONTH?

MONTH _____

SUNDAY	MONDAY	TUESDAY	WEDNESDAY
H	H	H	H
H	H	H	H
H	H	H	H
H	H	H	H
H	H	H	H

GOALS FOR THE MONTH

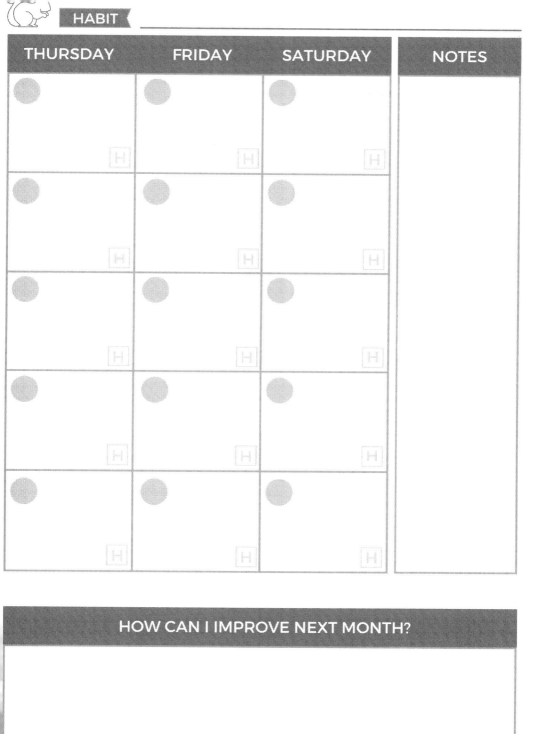

THURSDAY	FRIDAY	SATURDAY	NOTES
H	H	H	
H	H	H	
H	H	H	
H	H	H	
H	H	H	

HOW CAN I IMPROVE NEXT MONTH?

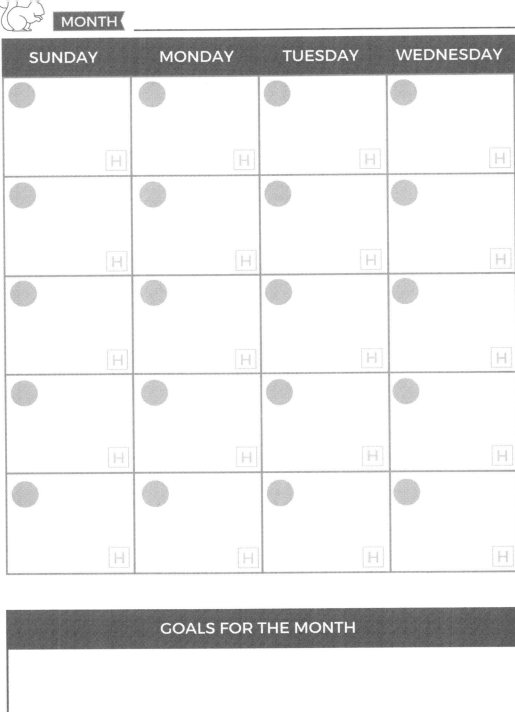

SUNDAY	MONDAY	TUESDAY	WEDNESDAY
H	H	H	H
H	H	H	H
H	H	H	H
H	H	H	H
H	H	H	H

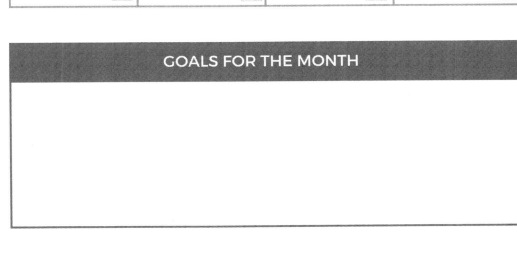

GOALS FOR THE MONTH

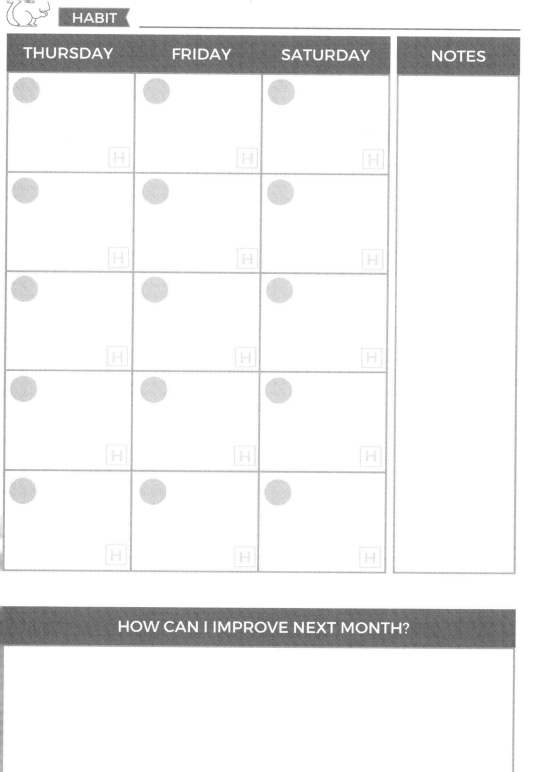

THURSDAY	FRIDAY	SATURDAY	NOTES

HOW CAN I IMPROVE NEXT MONTH?

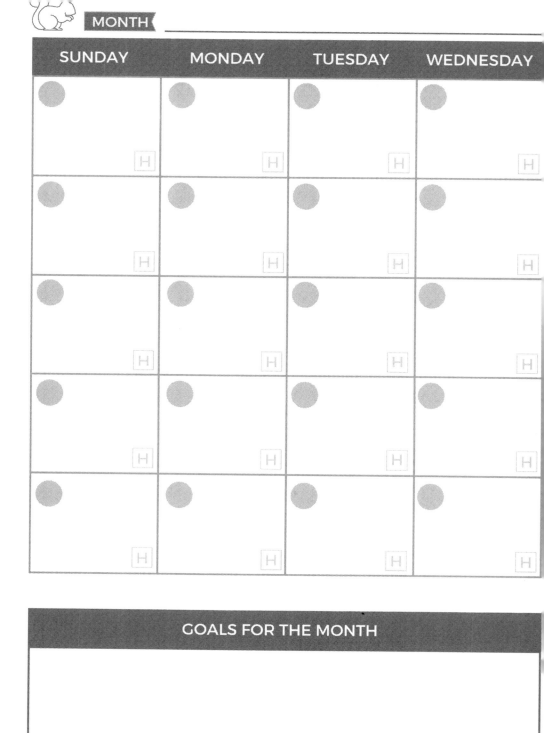

SUNDAY	MONDAY	TUESDAY	WEDNESDAY
H	H	H	H
H	H	H	H
H	H	H	H
H	H	H	H
H	H	H	H

GOALS FOR THE MONTH

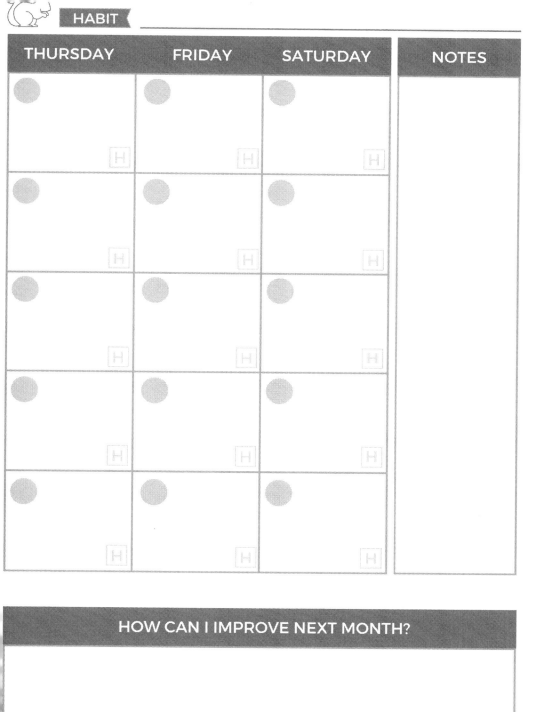

THURSDAY	FRIDAY	SATURDAY	NOTES
H	H	H	
H	H	H	
H	H	H	
H	H	H	
H	H	H	

HOW CAN I IMPROVE NEXT MONTH?

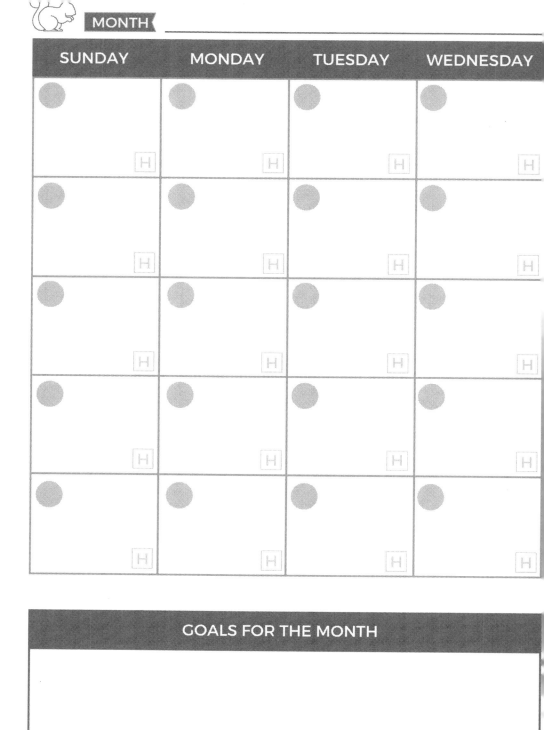

MONTH

SUNDAY	MONDAY	TUESDAY	WEDNESDAY
H	H	H	H
H	H	H	H
H	H	H	H
H	H	H	H
H	H	H	H

GOALS FOR THE MONTH

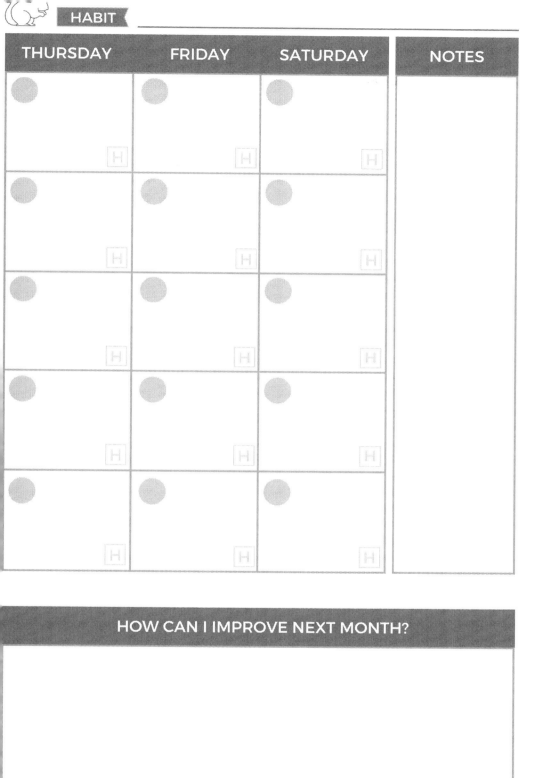

THURSDAY	FRIDAY	SATURDAY	NOTES
H	H	H	
H	H	H	
H	H	H	
H	H	H	
H	H	H	

HOW CAN I IMPROVE NEXT MONTH?

WEEK OF

Successes from last week

#1

#2

#3

#4

#5

Improvements for this week

#1

#2

#3

GOALS FOR THIS WEEK

WEEKLY AFFIRMATION

I AM GRATEFUL FOR....

weekly
long list

Today's Priorities

M

T

W

CALENDAR TASKS

CALENDAR TASKS

CALENDAR TASKS

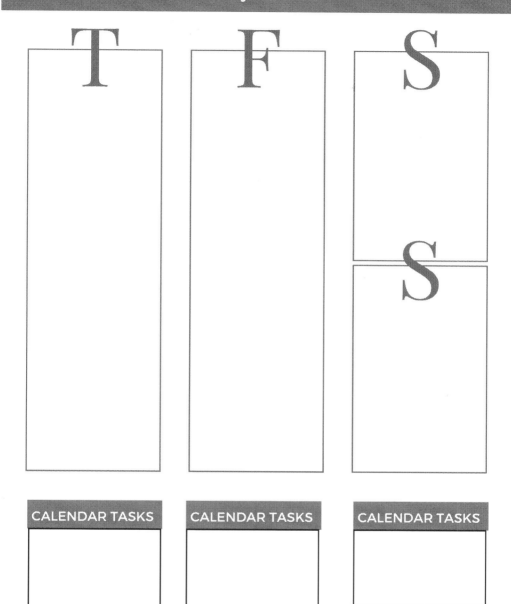

T

F

S

S

CALENDAR TASKS	CALENDAR TASKS	CALENDAR TASKS
		CALENDAR TASKS

Successes from last week

#1
#2
#3
#4
#5

Improvements for this week

#1
#2
#3

GOALS FOR THIS WEEK

WEEKLY AFFIRMATION

I AM GRATEFUL FOR....

weekly
long list

ONGOING PROJECTS/TASKS

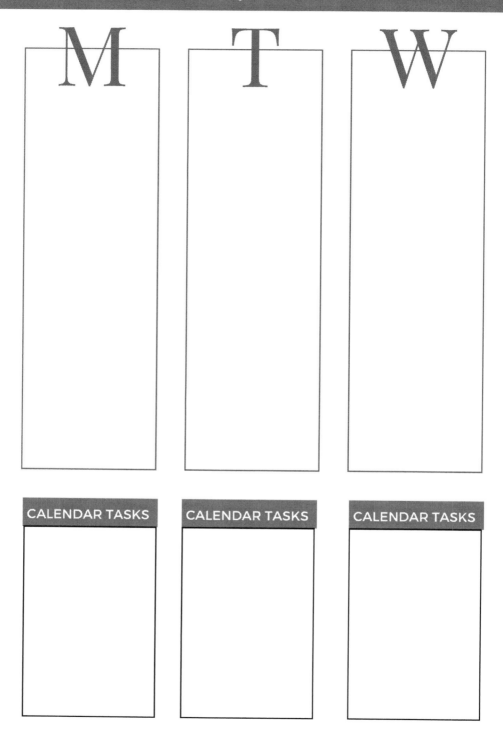

M

T

W

CALENDAR TASKS

CALENDAR TASKS

CALENDAR TASKS

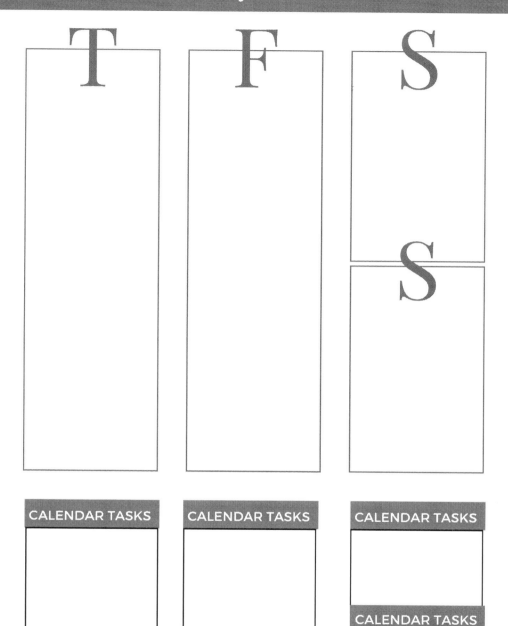

T

F

S

S

CALENDAR TASKS

CALENDAR TASKS

CALENDAR TASKS

CALENDAR TASKS

Successes from last week

#1

#2

#3

#4

#5

Improvements for this week

#1

#2

#3

GOALS FOR THIS WEEK

WEEKLY AFFIRMATION

I AM GRATEFUL FOR....

weekly
long list

ONGOING PROJECTS/TASKS

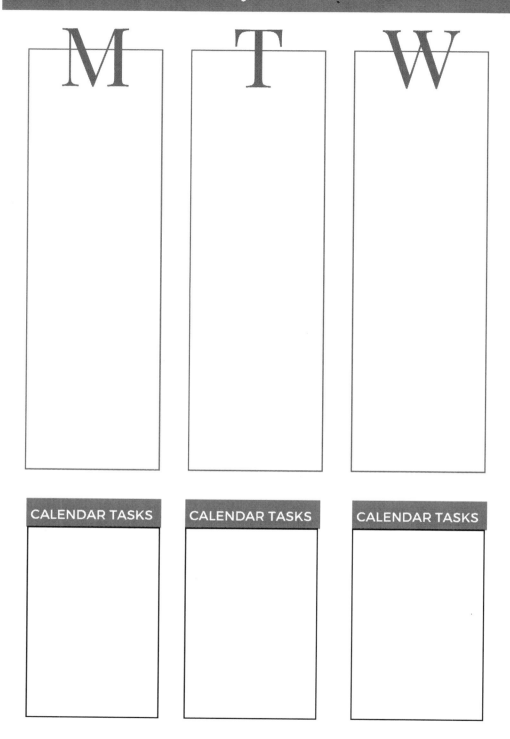

M

T

W

CALENDAR TASKS

CALENDAR TASKS

CALENDAR TASKS

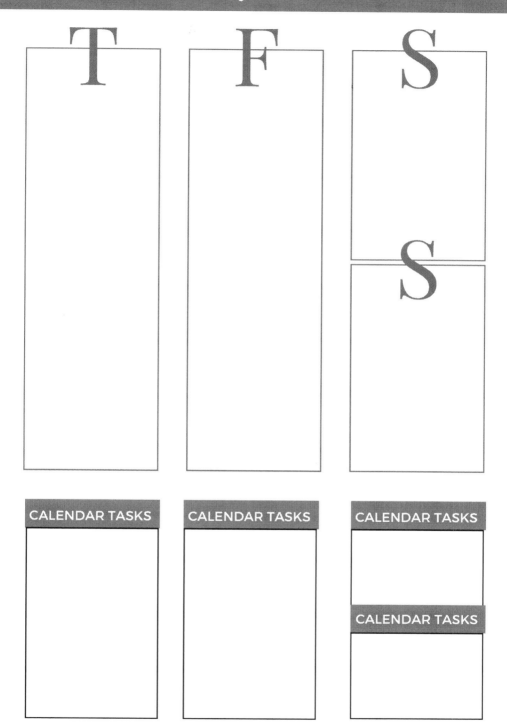

T

F

S

S

CALENDAR TASKS

CALENDAR TASKS

CALENDAR TASKS

CALENDAR TASKS

Successes from last week

#1

#2

#3

#4

#5

Improvements for this week

#1

#2

#3

GOALS FOR THIS WEEK

WEEKLY AFFIRMATION

I AM GRATEFUL FOR....

weekly
long list

M

T

W

CALENDAR TASKS

CALENDAR TASKS

CALENDAR TASKS

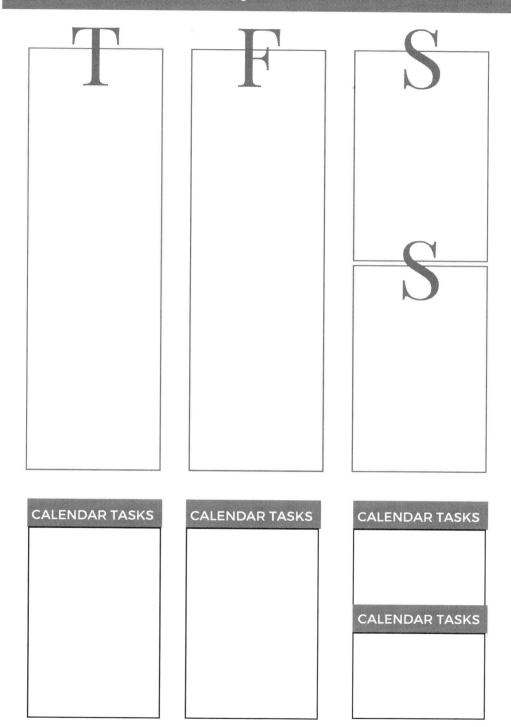

T

F

S

S

CALENDAR TASKS

CALENDAR TASKS

CALENDAR TASKS

CALENDAR TASKS

Successes from last week

#1

#2

#3

#4

#5

Improvements for this week

#1

#2

#3

GOALS FOR THIS WEEK

WEEKLY AFFIRMATION

I AM GRATEFUL FOR....

weekly
long list

ONGOING PROJECTS/TASKS

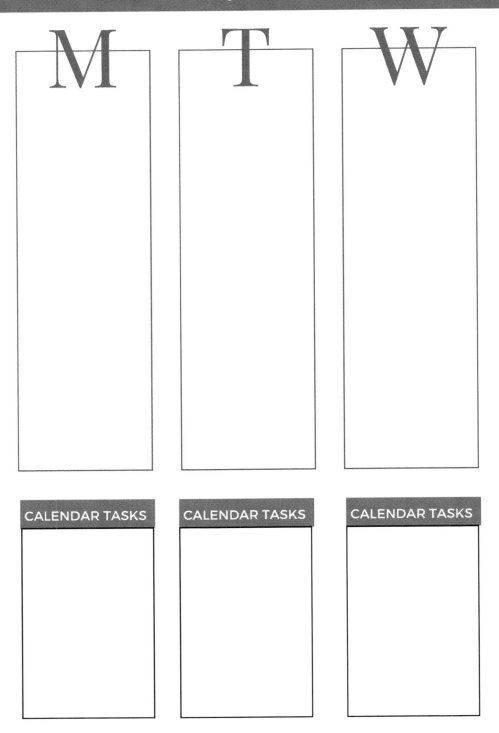

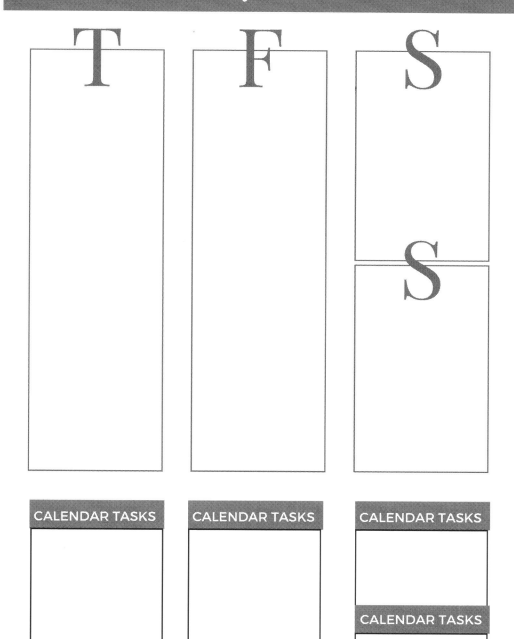

T

F

S

S

CALENDAR TASKS

CALENDAR TASKS

CALENDAR TASKS

CALENDAR TASKS

Successes from last week

#1
#2
#3
#4
#5

Improvements for this week

#1
#2
#3

GOALS FOR THIS WEEK

WEEKLY AFFIRMATION

I AM GRATEFUL FOR....

weekly
long list

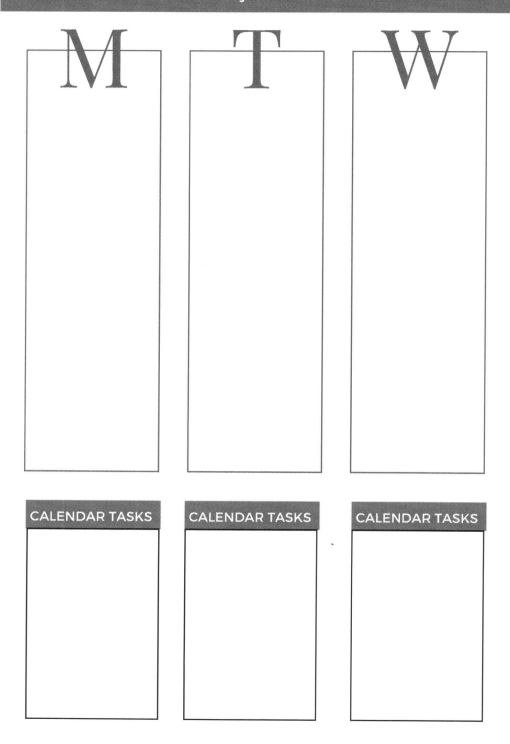

M

T

W

CALENDAR TASKS

CALENDAR TASKS

CALENDAR TASKS

T

F

S

S

CALENDAR TASKS

CALENDAR TASKS

CALENDAR TASKS

CALENDAR TASKS

 **WEEK OF**

Successes from last week

#1
#2
#3
#4
#5

Improvements for this week

#1
#2
#3

GOALS FOR THIS WEEK

WEEKLY AFFIRMATION

I AM GRATEFUL FOR....

weekly
long list

M

T

W

CALENDAR TASKS

CALENDAR TASKS

CALENDAR TASKS

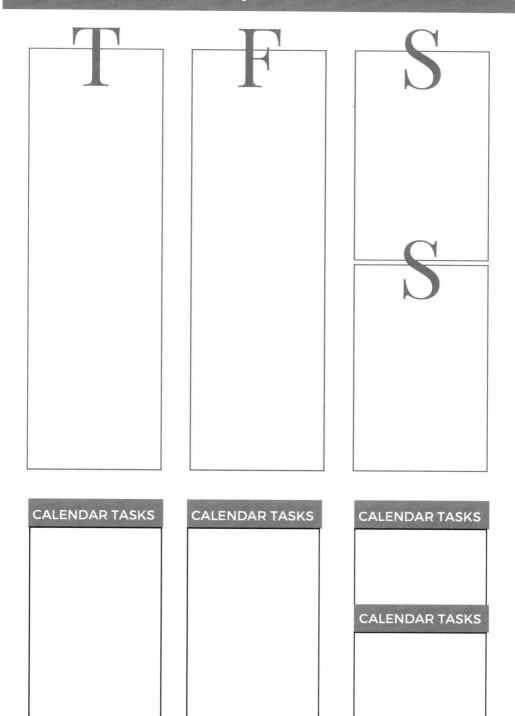

T

F

S

S

CALENDAR TASKS

CALENDAR TASKS

CALENDAR TASKS

CALENDAR TASKS

WEEK OF

Successes from last week

#1

#2

#3

#4

#5

Improvements for this week

#1

#2

#3

GOALS FOR THIS WEEK

WEEKLY AFFIRMATION

I AM GRATEFUL FOR....

weekly
long list

ONGOING PROJECTS/TASKS

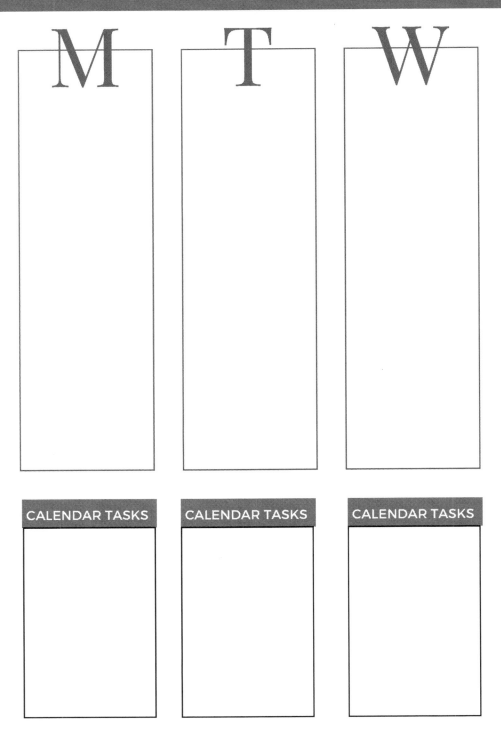

Today's Priorities

M

T

W

CALENDAR TASKS

CALENDAR TASKS

CALENDAR TASKS

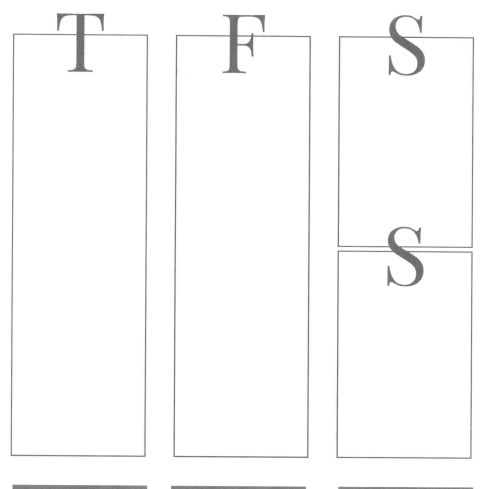

T	F	S
		S

CALENDAR TASKS	CALENDAR TASKS	CALENDAR TASKS
		CALENDAR TASKS

WEEK OF

Successes from last week

#1
#2
#3
#4
#5

Improvements for this week

#1
#2
#3

GOALS FOR THIS WEEK

WEEKLY AFFIRMATION

I AM GRATEFUL FOR....

weekly
long list

ONGOING PROJECTS/TASKS

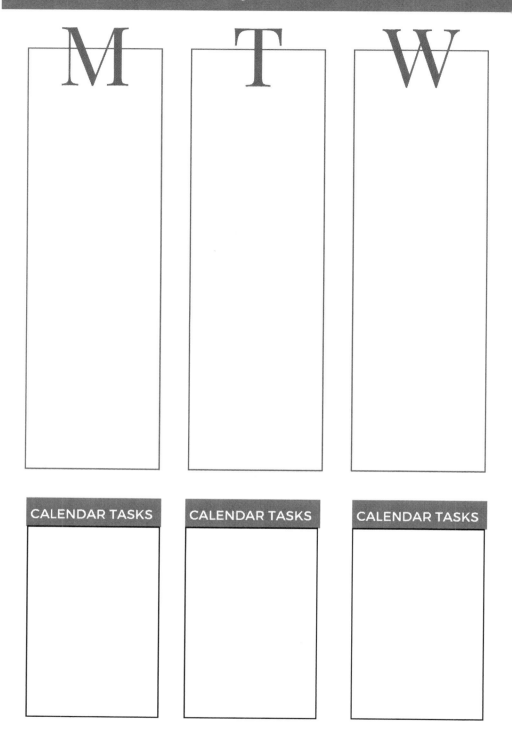

T

F

S

S

Successes from last week

#1

#2

#3

#4

#5

Improvements for this week

#1

#2

#3

GOALS FOR THIS WEEK

WEEKLY AFFIRMATION

I AM GRATEFUL FOR....

weekly
long list

M

T

W

CALENDAR TASKS

CALENDAR TASKS

CALENDAR TASKS

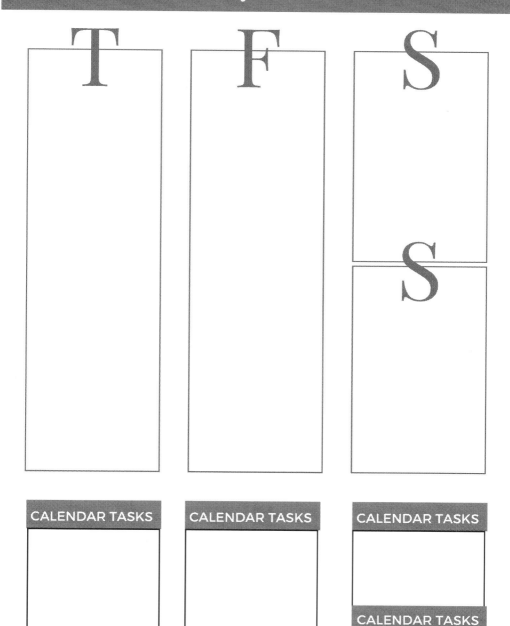

T

F

S

S

CALENDAR TASKS

CALENDAR TASKS

CALENDAR TASKS

CALENDAR TASKS

Successes from last week

#1

#2

#3

#4

#5

Improvements for this week

#1

#2

#3

GOALS FOR THIS WEEK

WEEKLY AFFIRMATION

I AM GRATEFUL FOR....

weekly
long list

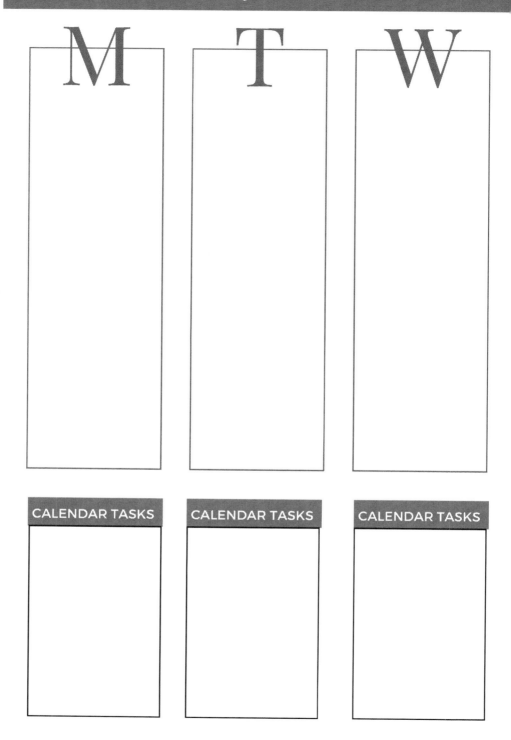

M

T

W

CALENDAR TASKS

CALENDAR TASKS

CALENDAR TASKS

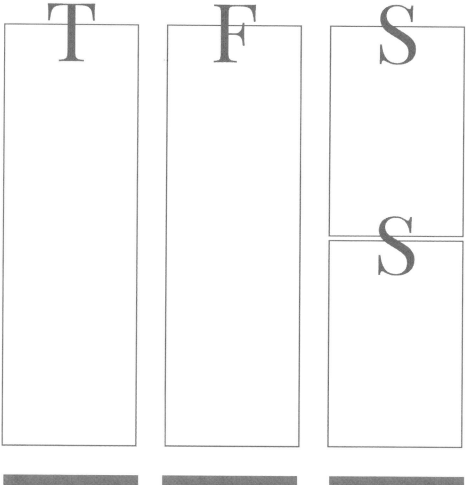

T

F

S

S

CALENDAR TASKS

CALENDAR TASKS

CALENDAR TASKS

CALENDAR TASKS

WEEK OF

Successes from last week
#1
#2
#3
#4
#5

Improvements for this week
#1
#2
#3

GOALS FOR THIS WEEK

WEEKLY AFFIRMATION

I AM GRATEFUL FOR....

weekly
long list

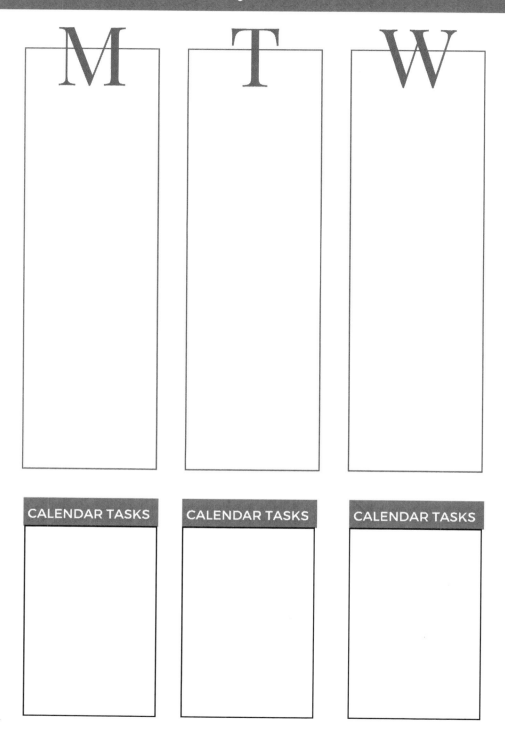

M

T

W

CALENDAR TASKS

CALENDAR TASKS

CALENDAR TASKS

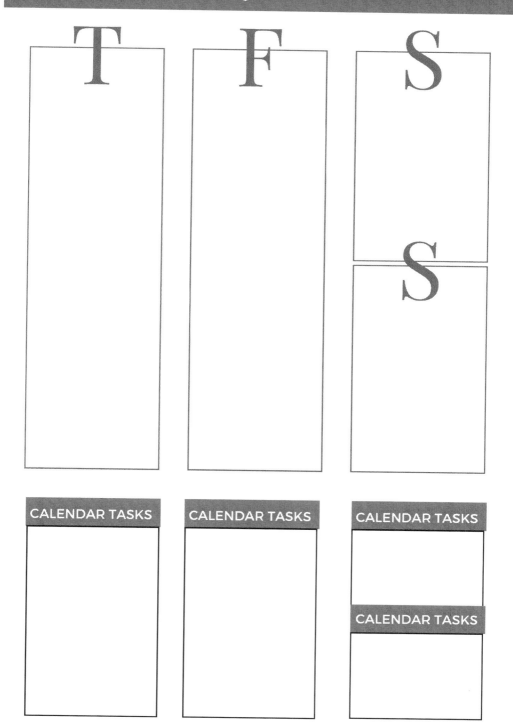

T

F

S

S

CALENDAR TASKS

CALENDAR TASKS

CALENDAR TASKS

CALENDAR TASKS

Successes from last week

#1

#2

#3

#4

#5

Improvements for this week

#1

#2

#3

GOALS FOR THIS WEEK

WEEKLY AFFIRMATION

I AM GRATEFUL FOR....

weekly
long list

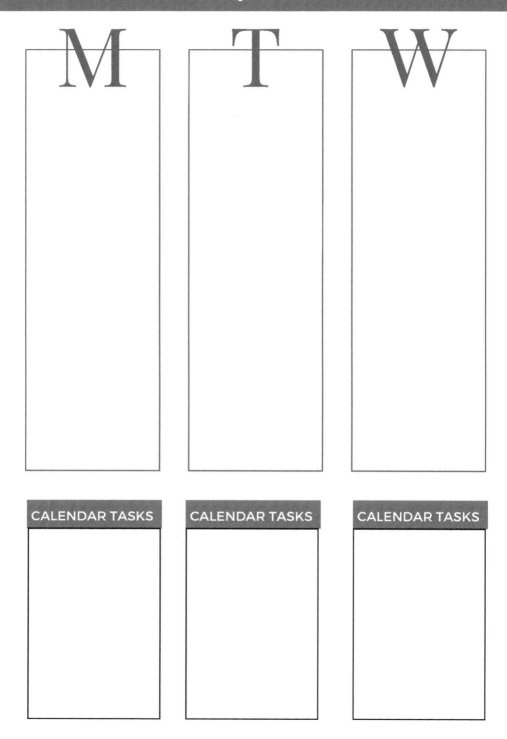

M

T

W

CALENDAR TASKS

CALENDAR TASKS

CALENDAR TASKS

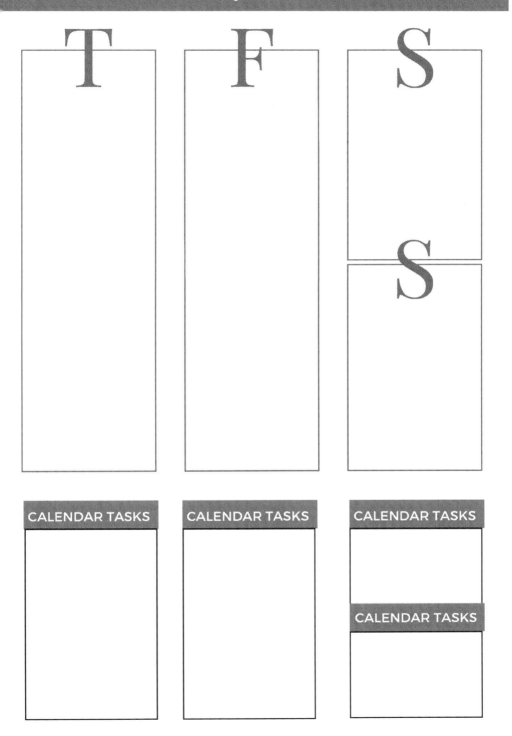

T

F

S

S

CALENDAR TASKS

CALENDAR TASKS

CALENDAR TASKS

CALENDAR TASKS

Successes from last week

#1

#2

#3

#4

#5

Improvements for this week

#1

#2

#3

GOALS FOR THIS WEEK

WEEKLY AFFIRMATION

I AM GRATEFUL FOR....

weekly
long list

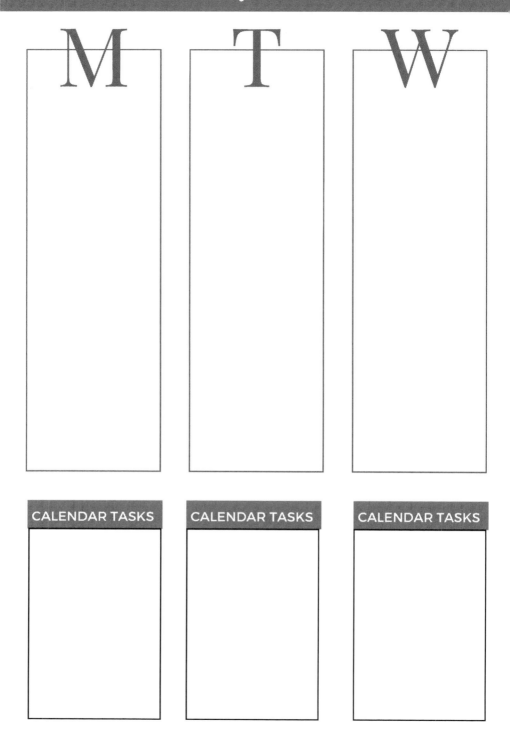

M
T
W

CALENDAR TASKS
CALENDAR TASKS
CALENDAR TASKS

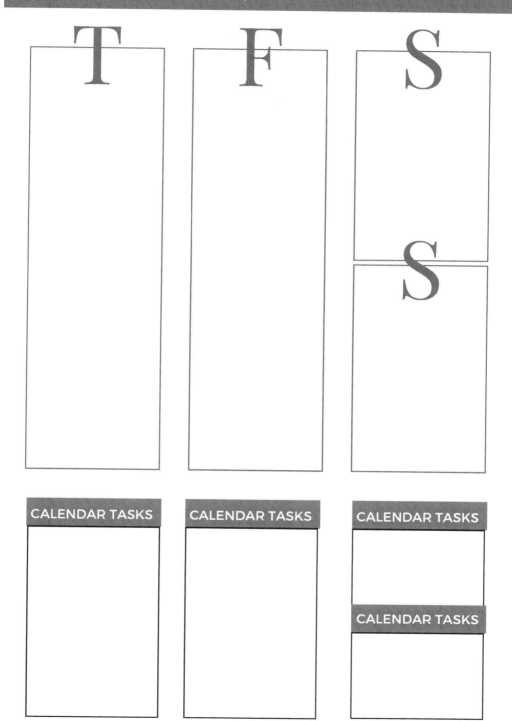

T

F

S

S

CALENDAR TASKS

CALENDAR TASKS

CALENDAR TASKS

CALENDAR TASKS

Successes from last week

#1

#2

#3

#4

#5

Improvements for this week

#1

#2

#3

GOALS FOR THIS WEEK

WEEKLY AFFIRMATION

I AM GRATEFUL FOR....

weekly
long list

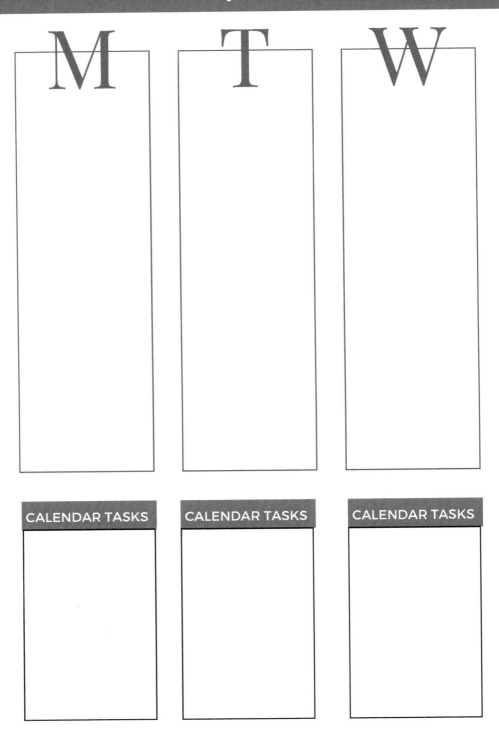

M

T

W

CALENDAR TASKS

CALENDAR TASKS

CALENDAR TASKS

T

F

S

S

CALENDAR TASKS

CALENDAR TASKS

CALENDAR TASKS

CALENDAR TASKS

WEEK OF

Successes from last week

#1
#2
#3
#4
#5

Improvements for this week

#1
#2
#3

GOALS FOR THIS WEEK

WEEKLY AFFIRMATION

I AM GRATEFUL FOR....

weekly
long list

ONGOING PROJECTS/TASKS

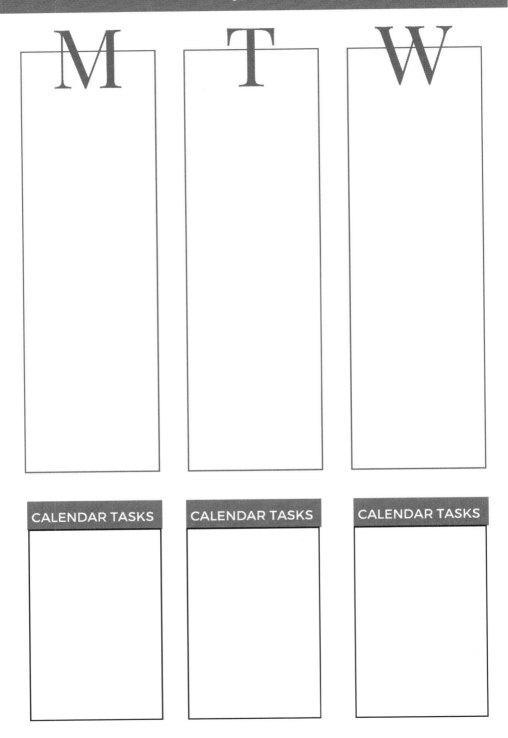

M

T

W

CALENDAR TASKS

CALENDAR TASKS

CALENDAR TASKS

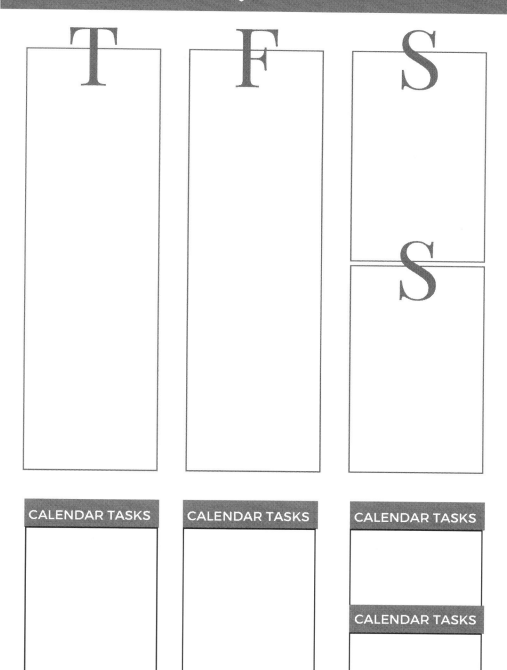

T

F

S

S

CALENDAR TASKS

CALENDAR TASKS

CALENDAR TASKS

CALENDAR TASKS

Successes from last week

#1

#2

#3

#4

#5

Improvements for this week

#1

#2

#3

GOALS FOR THIS WEEK

WEEKLY AFFIRMATION

I AM GRATEFUL FOR....

weekly
long list

Today's Priorities

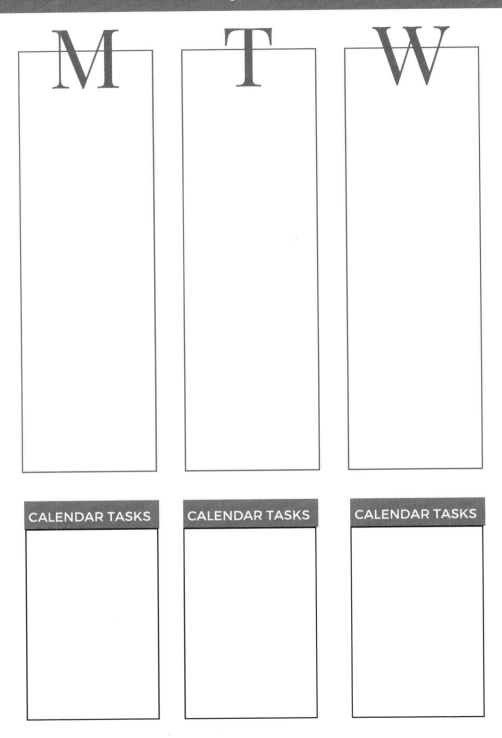

M   T   W

CALENDAR TASKS   CALENDAR TASKS   CALENDAR TASKS

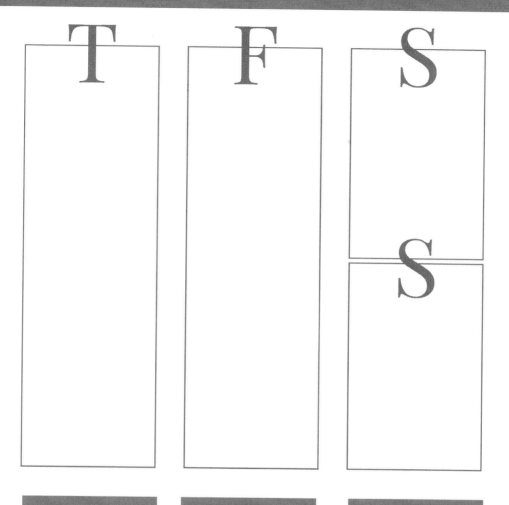

T

F

S

S

 **WEEK OF**

Successes from last week

#1

#2

#3

#4

#5

Improvements for this week

#1

#2

#3

GOALS FOR THIS WEEK

WEEKLY AFFIRMATION

I AM GRATEFUL FOR....

weekly
long list

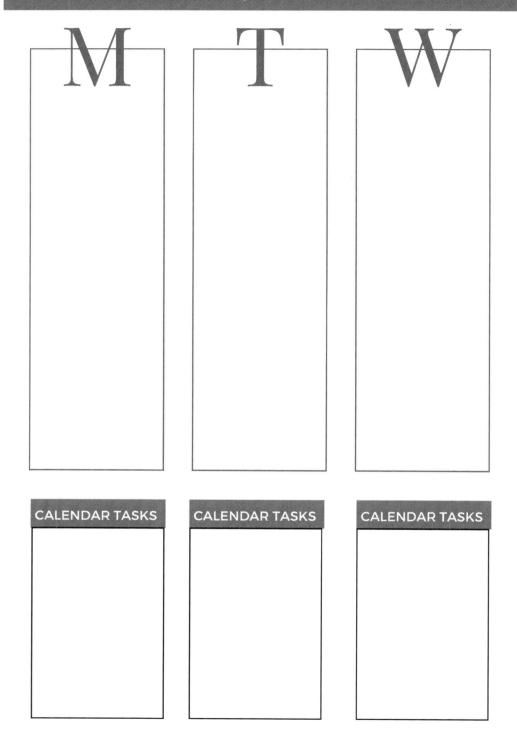

M

T

W

CALENDAR TASKS

CALENDAR TASKS

CALENDAR TASKS

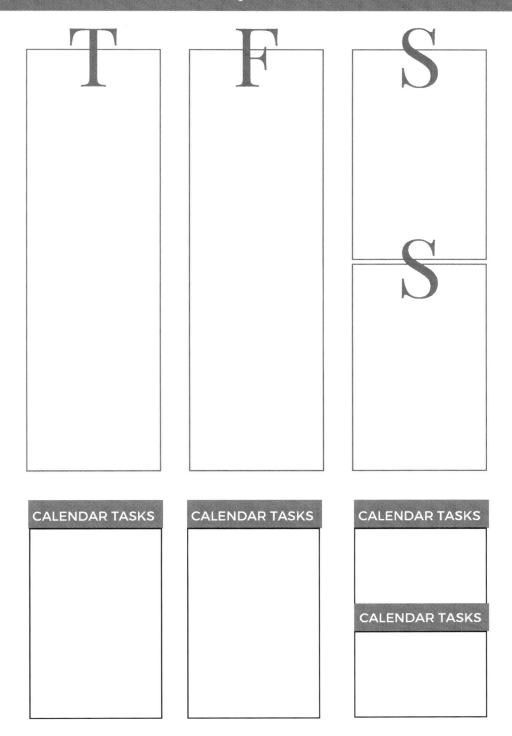

Successes from last week

#1

#2

#3

#4

#5

Improvements for this week

#1

#2

#3

GOALS FOR THIS WEEK

WEEKLY AFFIRMATION

I AM GRATEFUL FOR....

weekly
long list

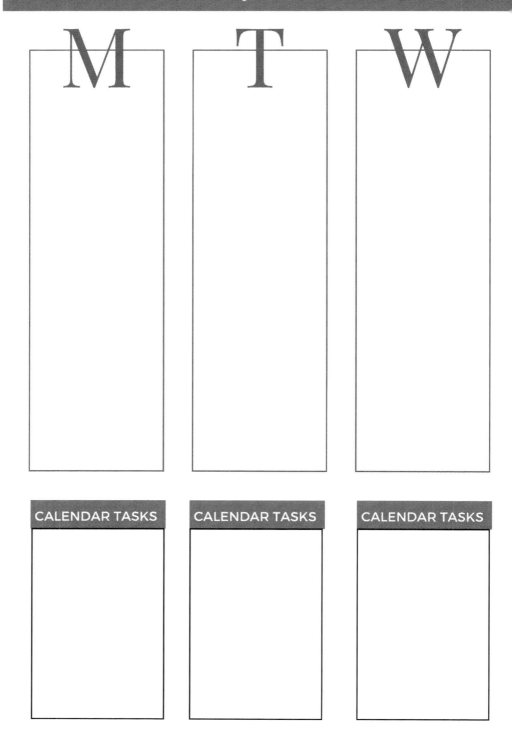

M

T

W

CALENDAR TASKS

CALENDAR TASKS

CALENDAR TASKS

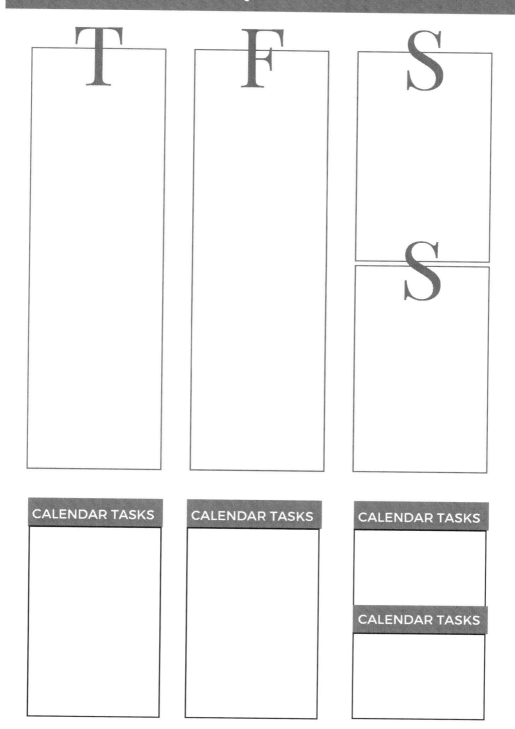

T

F

S

S

CALENDAR TASKS

CALENDAR TASKS

CALENDAR TASKS

CALENDAR TASKS

 **WEEK OF**

Successes from last week

#1
#2
#3
#4
#5

Improvements for this week

#1
#2
#3

GOALS FOR THIS WEEK

WEEKLY AFFIRMATION

I AM GRATEFUL FOR....

weekly
long list

ONGOING PROJECTS/TASKS

M   T   W

CALENDAR TASKS

CALENDAR TASKS

CALENDAR TASKS

Today's Priorities

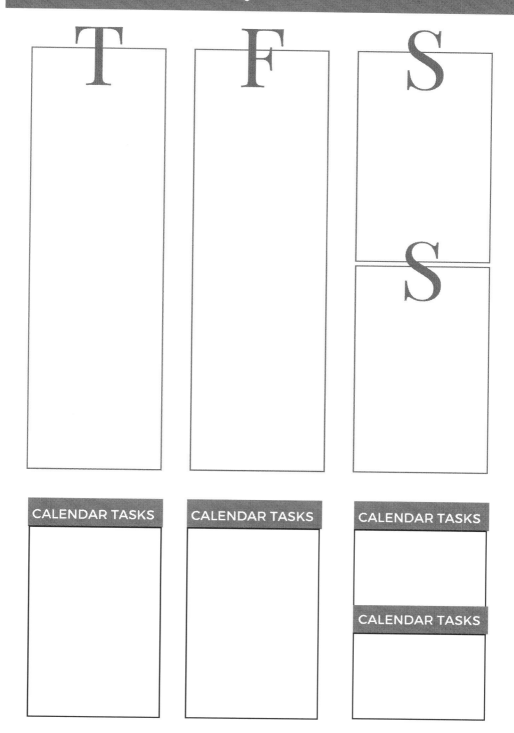

T

F

S

S

CALENDAR TASKS

CALENDAR TASKS

CALENDAR TASKS

CALENDAR TASKS

WEEK OF

Successes from last week

#1
#2
#3
#4
#5

Improvements for this week

#1
#2
#3

GOALS FOR THIS WEEK

WEEKLY AFFIRMATION

I AM GRATEFUL FOR....

weekly
long list

ONGOING PROJECTS/TASKS

M

T

W

CALENDAR TASKS

CALENDAR TASKS

CALENDAR TASKS

Today's Priorities

T

F

S

S

CALENDAR TASKS

CALENDAR TASKS

CALENDAR TASKS

CALENDAR TASKS

Successes from last week

#1
#2
#3
#4
#5

Improvements for this week

#1
#2
#3

GOALS FOR THIS WEEK

WEEKLY AFFIRMATION

I AM GRATEFUL FOR....

weekly
long list

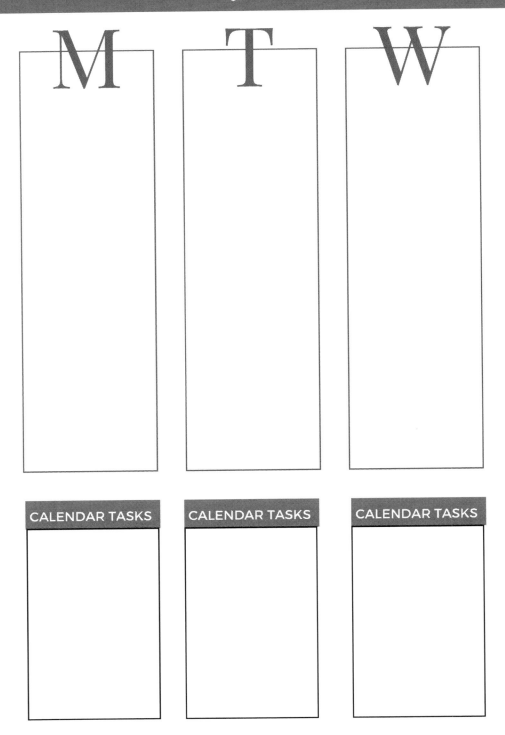

M   T   W

CALENDAR TASKS   CALENDAR TASKS   CALENDAR TASKS

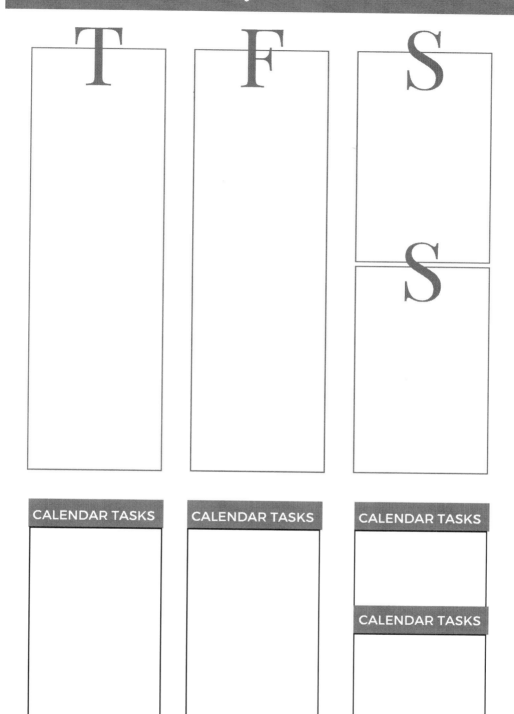

T

F

S

S

CALENDAR TASKS

CALENDAR TASKS

CALENDAR TASKS

CALENDAR TASKS

WEEK OF

Successes from last week

#1

#2

#3

#4

#5

Improvements for this week

#1

#2

#3

GOALS FOR THIS WEEK

WEEKLY AFFIRMATION

I AM GRATEFUL FOR....

weekly
long list

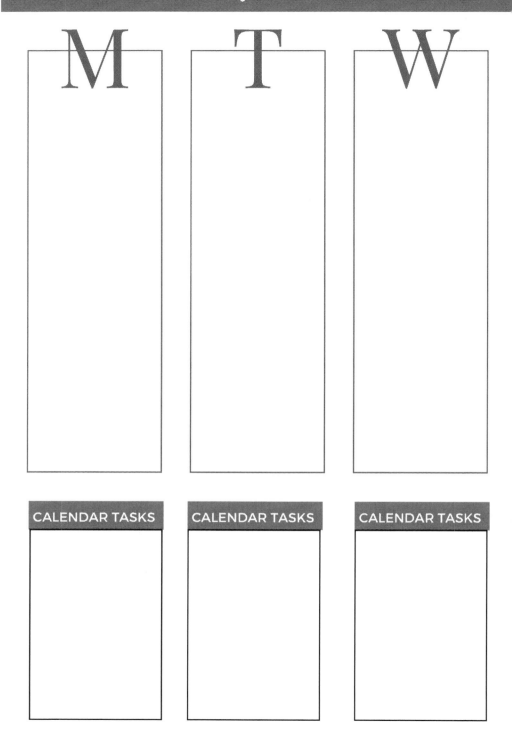

Today's Priorities

M

T

W

CALENDAR TASKS

CALENDAR TASKS

CALENDAR TASKS

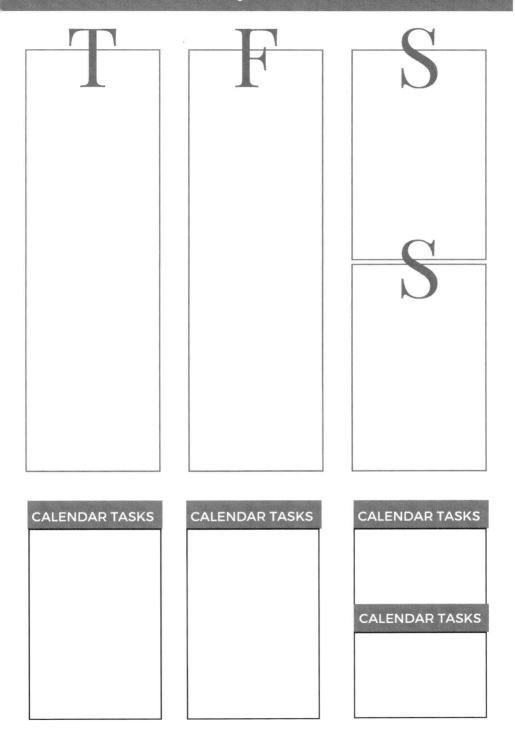

T

F

S

S

CALENDAR TASKS

CALENDAR TASKS

CALENDAR TASKS

CALENDAR TASKS

Successes from last week

#1

#2

#3

#4

#5

Improvements for this week

#1

#2

#3

GOALS FOR THIS WEEK

WEEKLY AFFIRMATION

I AM GRATEFUL FOR....

weekly
long list

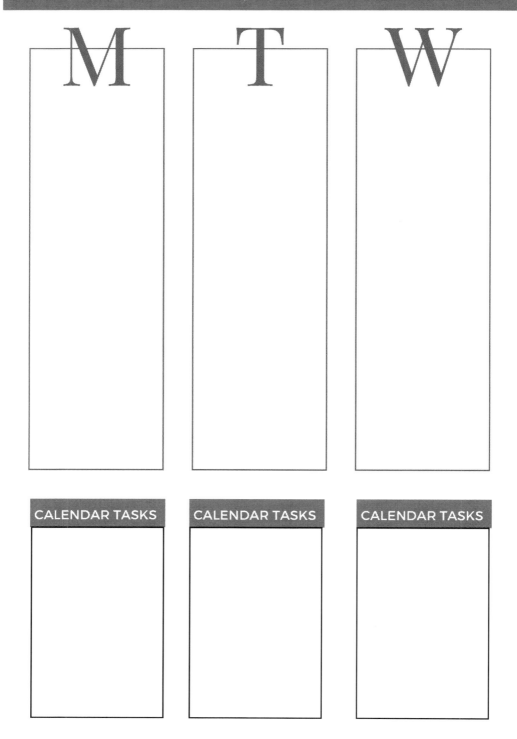

M

T

W

CALENDAR TASKS

CALENDAR TASKS

CALENDAR TASKS

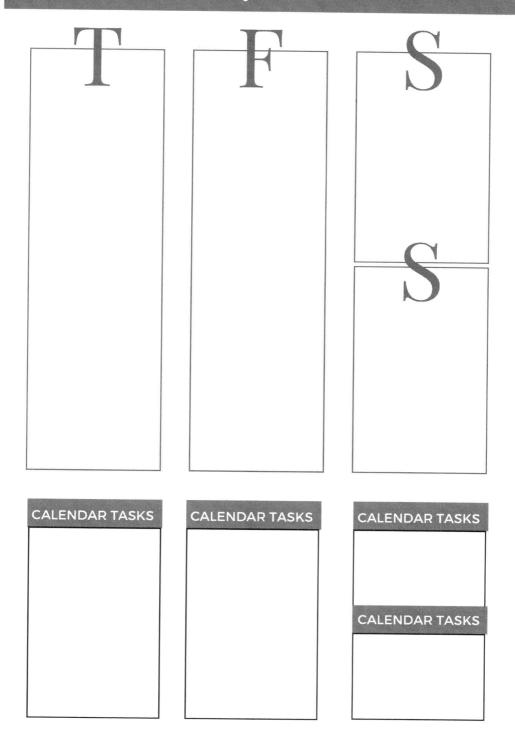

WEEK OF

Successes from last week

#1
#2
#3
#4
#5

Improvements for this week

#1
#2
#3

GOALS FOR THIS WEEK

WEEKLY AFFIRMATION

I AM GRATEFUL FOR....

weekly
long list

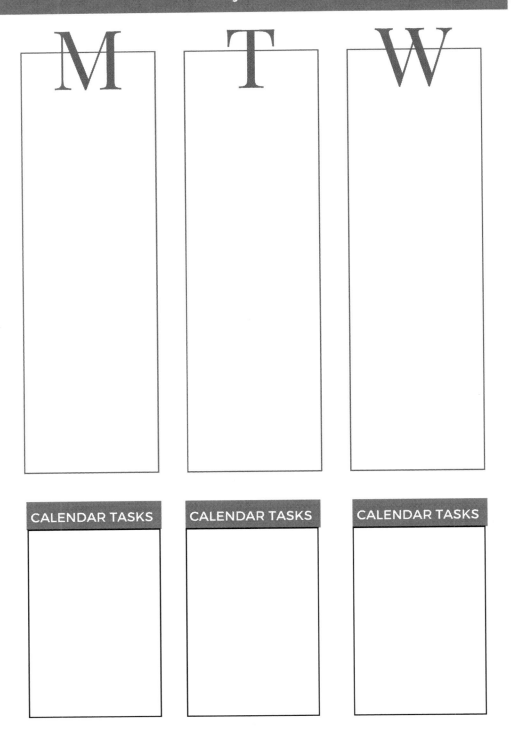

M

T

W

CALENDAR TASKS

CALENDAR TASKS

CALENDAR TASKS

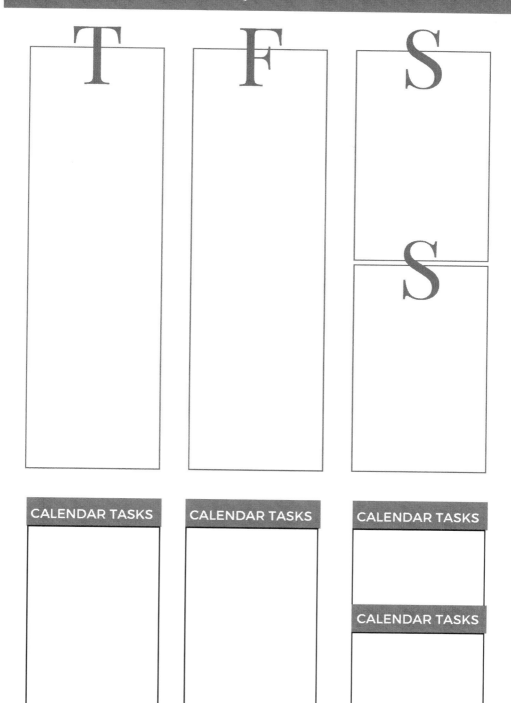

T

F

S

S

CALENDAR TASKS

CALENDAR TASKS

CALENDAR TASKS

CALENDAR TASKS

Successes from last week

#1
#2
#3
#4
#5

Improvements for this week

#1
#2
#3

GOALS FOR THIS WEEK

WEEKLY AFFIRMATION

I AM GRATEFUL FOR....

weekly
long list

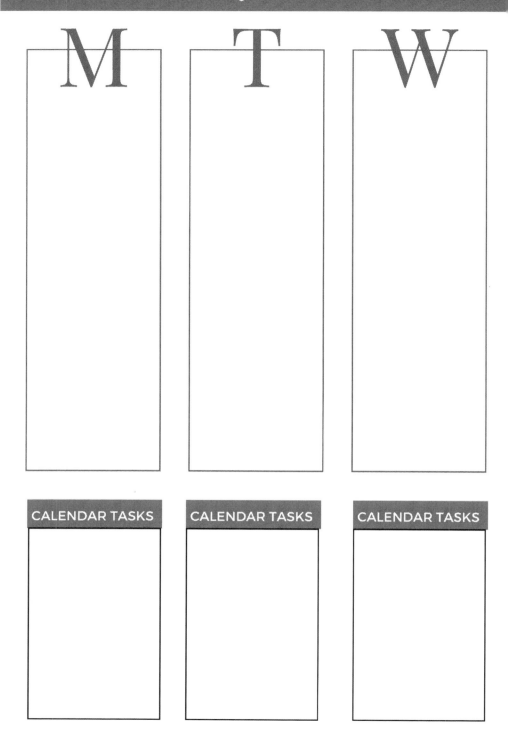

M

T

W

CALENDAR TASKS

CALENDAR TASKS

CALENDAR TASKS

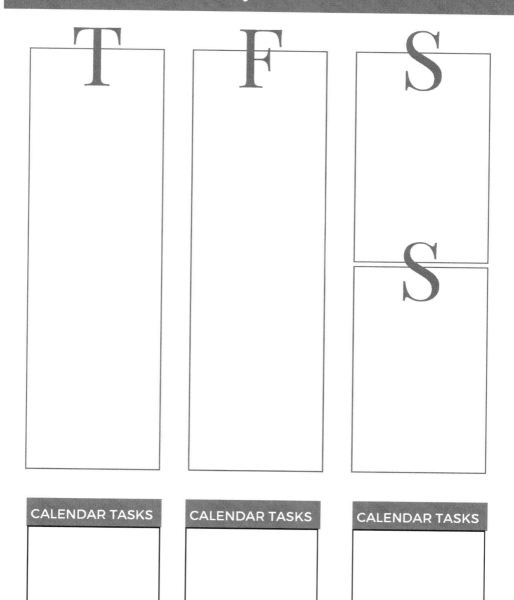

T

F

S

S

CALENDAR TASKS

CALENDAR TASKS

CALENDAR TASKS

CALENDAR TASKS

IF I HAD A DOLLAR FOR EVERY TIME I GOT DISTRACTED,

oh, look a squirrel!

I DON'T HAVE A SHORT ATTENTION SPAN, I JUST...

oh, look a squirrel!

Made in the USA
Monee, IL
21 March 2022